Jules

The Autonomous Artificial Intelligence That Codes, Fixes, and Transforms Development

How Google's Groundbreaking AI Coding Assistant Is Reinventing the Developer's Workflow

Joe E. Grayson

Table of Contents

Introduction

Artificial intelligence is no longer a distant dream in the realm of software development. It has swiftly evolved from a theoretical concept to a transformative force reshaping the way developers approach coding. From automated bug detection to intelligent code suggestions, AI has become an invaluable asset in every developer's toolkit. In this landscape, one AI tool stands out: Jules.

Jules is not just another coding assistant. It is an autonomous artificial intelligence designed to take on some of the most time-consuming and error-prone tasks in software development. Unlike its predecessors, which merely offered suggestions or simple fixes, Jules operates as an independent agent within a developer's workflow, capable of autonomously analyzing, fixing, and optimizing code with minimal human intervention. By seamlessly integrating into existing development environments like GitHub, Jules significantly enhances productivity and allows developers to focus on more complex, creative aspects of their work.

The goal of this book is to provide a comprehensive, in-depth exploration of Jules—what it is, how it works, and why it represents a groundbreaking advancement in AI-assisted coding. We will explore how Jules operates, its capabilities, and its real-world applications, highlighting the profound impact it's having on software development workflows. This book aims to offer developers, tech enthusiasts, and industry professionals a deep understanding of how Jules is changing the game and why it is poised to be a central figure in the future of coding.

As AI continues to evolve, its role in software development becomes ever more critical. From automating repetitive tasks to enhancing code quality and speeding up development cycles, AI tools like Jules are making development processes faster, more efficient, and more cost-effective. The broader development community must understand these shifts, as they will not only influence the way software is created but also the future careers of developers themselves. Embracing AI tools like Jules isn't just a trend—it's an essential step towards staying competitive and pushing the boundaries of what is possible in software development.

Chapter 1: Understanding the Evolution of AI Coding Assistants

The journey of AI in software development began with a relatively simple goal: to enhance productivity and reduce the manual burden on developers. In the early days, software development tools were basic but indispensable—things like compilers, debuggers, and version control systems. These tools helped coders ensure their programs ran correctly, allowed them to track changes, and facilitated collaboration. While immensely helpful, these tools still required significant human effort to detect bugs, optimize code, and manage revisions. There was little automation beyond the basic functions they offered.

As programming languages grew more complex, so did the challenges that developers faced. Debugging, for instance, became an increasingly time-consuming task. It wasn't just about finding syntax errors but dealing with logical issues, performance bottlenecks, and security vulnerabilities. This growing complexity called for more advanced tools—ones that could assist not only in error detection but also in identifying potential improvements to the code. Enter the early days of "coding assistants."

Early coding assistants were often rudimentary and functioned mainly as syntax checkers or code completion tools. Tools like Microsoft Visual Studio's IntelliSense, for example, helped developers by providing code suggestions and completing syntax based on context. These tools didn't understand the code; they simply followed predefined rules to speed up the coding process.

While helpful, they still left much of the heavy lifting to the developer, offering little in terms of autonomous decision-making or deep understanding of the code's structure and purpose.

The next step in the evolution came with the introduction of machine learning and natural language processing into coding assistants. These advancements enabled assistants to go beyond simple suggestions and actually begin to "understand" the code—at least in a limited way. GitHub Copilot, for example, introduced by OpenAI and GitHub, allowed developers to type a prompt and receive code suggestions that fit contextually with their intent. These suggestions were informed by a large corpus of existing code, making them more relevant than previous tools. However, they still required significant input from developers to be useful and often needed human validation before any change could be made.

This is where AI assistants like Jules stand apart. Unlike traditional coding assistants, Jules isn't just offering suggestions; it is taking action autonomously. Built on the advanced Gemini 2.0 platform, Jules has the ability to analyze entire codebases, detect bugs, propose solutions, and even implement fixes—all without continuous human intervention. What sets Jules apart is its deeper integration into developer workflows. Rather than being an add-on that offers simple suggestions, Jules operates as a fully integrated, autonomous agent that works directly within platforms like GitHub. This allows Jules to analyze complex code and manage updates across multiple files simultaneously, executing comprehensive fixes with minimal human oversight.

Traditional tools were limited in scope—they could help with minor tasks but still required developers to manage the bigger picture. On the other hand, AI assistants like Jules operate as independent agents, making them far more efficient. They don't just "assist" in the traditional sense of providing suggestions; they take responsibility for tasks like bug fixing, code optimization, and preparing pull requests—tasks that once required significant developer time and attention. Jules can analyze a codebase as a whole, identify inconsistencies, propose solutions, and execute fixes autonomously. Its ability to seamlessly integrate with a developer's existing workflow without disrupting the process is another game-changer. Where traditional tools demanded human oversight at every step, Jules allows developers to review and approve actions, ensuring control without constant intervention.

What makes AI assistants like Jules so different is their capacity to handle complexity at scale. Traditional tools may have offered isolated fixes, but they couldn't handle the multifaceted nature of real-world development projects. Jules, however, is built to manage the intricate, large-scale demands of modern software development. With the ability to analyze, detect, fix, and optimize code at an unprecedented level, Jules is redefining what it means to assist developers. In this new era, AI is no longer a passive tool—it's an active participant, working alongside human developers to accelerate the development process and improve the quality of software in ways never before possible.

In the fast-paced world of software development, developers are constantly navigating a labyrinth of challenges that can slow progress, increase costs, and affect the overall quality of their work. One of the most persistent hurdles is **bug fixing**. No matter how skilled a developer is, bugs are an inevitable part of the coding process. Identifying and resolving bugs can be a time-consuming and frustrating task, often involving hours of sifting through lines of code, running tests, and debugging in isolation. Even with the best tools, finding the root cause of a bug can feel like searching for a needle in a haystack, especially in large, complex projects where one small error can ripple through and cause numerous issues.

Time consumption is another major struggle. Developers often find themselves spending significant portions of their time on repetitive, mundane tasks. From fixing simple syntax errors to managing complex code revisions, these tasks consume valuable hours that could otherwise be spent on more creative and high-impact work. Over time, this adds up, leading to delayed project timelines and, in some cases, cost overruns. A developer's time is their most valuable resource, and yet much of it is drained by routine maintenance, bug fixes, and ensuring compatibility across platforms.

Code quality also presents a significant challenge. Writing code that is efficient, maintainable, and scalable requires expertise and experience. Even experienced developers can struggle with keeping their code clean and free of vulnerabilities. Bugs can emerge not just from mistakes in logic but from poor code structure, outdated practices, or even conflicting dependencies. Ensuring that code is consistently high-quality, readable, and well-documented requires constant attention to detail—a task that can be overwhelming when juggling multiple aspects of a project.

These persistent challenges—bug fixing, time consumption, and code quality—are all part of the larger equation of **efficiency** in software development. As much as developers are highly skilled, their ability to manage these tasks is limited by human capacity. As a result, the development cycle becomes longer, more error-prone, and less efficient. This is where AI-driven tools like Jules come into play, offering solutions that can not only alleviate these struggles but also transform the way software is developed.

What makes **Jules** so special is its ability to address these core issues in ways that traditional tools cannot. Unlike basic coding assistants or bug-tracking software, Jules goes beyond offering suggestions. It operates as a fully autonomous agent, seamlessly integrated into platforms like GitHub, and capable of analyzing, fixing, and optimizing code without constant human supervision. Rather than simply identifying bugs or offering snippets of code, Jules can create comprehensive repair plans for complex codebases, automating fixes across multiple files simultaneously. This level of autonomy allows developers to save valuable time by reducing the need for manual intervention.

One of the key innovations of Jules is its ability to not only detect bugs but also offer and implement solutions without human input at every step. Traditional coding assistants might suggest a fix for a bug, but it is up to the developer to apply it, test it, and ensure it works in the broader context of the code. Jules, however, acts like a full-fledged team member. It doesn't just point out the problem; it actively proposes and executes fixes, reducing the time spent on debugging. This autonomy streamlines development processes, allowing developers to focus on more high-level tasks that require human creativity and judgment.

Another feature that sets Jules apart is its deep **understanding of codebases**. Traditional tools can only analyze code in isolation, without considering the broader architecture of the project. Jules, on the other hand, can analyze entire codebases and understand the interdependencies between files. This ability allows Jules to provide more contextually relevant fixes and optimizations, ensuring that changes made in one part of the code don't inadvertently break other areas of the project.

In addition, Jules integrates seamlessly into existing workflows. This means that developers don't have to abandon their familiar tools or processes. Instead, they can continue working within platforms like GitHub while allowing Jules to handle routine tasks like bug fixing, pull requests, and code review. This integration allows for greater flexibility and less disruption, making it easier for teams to adopt AI into their development cycles without a steep learning curve.

Ultimately, Jules represents a significant leap forward in AI-powered coding assistants. It is not just a tool that supports developers—it's an autonomous agent capable of reducing the time spent on repetitive tasks, enhancing the quality of code, and improving the overall efficiency of the development process. With its advanced features and seamless integration, Jules is poised to become a central figure in the world of software development, helping developers to not only write better code but to write it faster and more effectively than ever before.

Chapter 2: Jules' Architecture and the Power of Gemini 2.0

At the heart of **Jules** lies the powerful **Gemini 2.0 platform**, a cutting-edge technology that powers the AI's remarkable capabilities. Gemini 2.0 represents a significant leap forward in artificial intelligence architecture, designed specifically to tackle the complexities of modern software development. Unlike previous platforms that simply applied basic AI models for limited tasks, Gemini 2.0 combines a range of advanced techniques, including machine learning, deep learning, and natural language processing, to create a system that is capable of understanding, analyzing, and improving code on a level far beyond anything seen before.

The **architecture of Gemini 2.0** is built to handle the vast amounts of data and intricate processes involved in software development. At its core, Gemini 2.0 uses advanced neural networks that allow it to learn and adapt over time. These neural networks are designed to understand both the structure and context of code, meaning that they can perform tasks not only based on syntax but also on the underlying logic and functionality. This is crucial because code isn't just a series of instructions; it's a complex web of interconnected elements that must work together cohesively. Gemini 2.0's architecture enables it to grasp these interdependencies and provide solutions that are contextually aware.

One of the defining features of Gemini 2.0 is its ability to work across multiple layers of a codebase. It can analyze not only individual lines of code but entire projects, including dependencies, libraries, and frameworks, understanding the bigger picture in which a piece of code operates. This ability to evaluate code at such a comprehensive level is what enables **Jules** to perform fixes autonomously, without needing continuous developer input. Whether it's fixing bugs, refactoring code, or suggesting optimizations, Gemini 2.0 ensures that the solutions provided are not just superficial fixes but long-term, scalable improvements.

Additionally, Gemini 2.0 is designed for seamless integration with existing tools. It works directly within platforms like GitHub, where it can automatically pull in code, analyze it, and make the necessary changes. This integration ensures that developers don't have to step outside of their familiar environments, making it easier for teams to adopt and incorporate AI without disrupting their workflow. With its advanced architecture, Gemini 2.0 empowers **Jules** to analyze large, complex codebases with ease, providing developers with a tool that can handle even the most demanding software projects.

Jules' ability to autonomously fix code and offer actionable suggestions is powered by its underlying **machine learning algorithms** and **neural networks**, which work together in a highly sophisticated way. The key to understanding how Jules operates lies in how it processes and learns from the vast amounts of data it encounters in the development environment.

At its core, **machine learning** allows Jules to identify patterns in code, learn from previous data, and improve its performance over time. When a developer writes code, there are often patterns in how certain bugs occur or how common problems are solved. By training on millions of code samples, Jules learns to recognize these patterns and apply solutions in real-time. This ability to learn from data and adjust its behavior makes Jules much more than a simple automation tool—it makes it an intelligent assistant capable of understanding complex problems and providing relevant solutions.

Neural networks play a crucial role in enabling Jules to perform advanced tasks like bug fixing and code optimization. These deep learning models allow Jules to understand the context of a piece of code, not just the syntax. For example, when Jules encounters a bug, it doesn't simply look for a syntax error or flag an obvious mistake. Instead, it uses its neural networks to understand the logic of the code and identify more subtle issues, such as performance bottlenecks or security vulnerabilities. By processing code through multiple layers of neural networks, Jules can detect these more intricate problems, which might go unnoticed by a human developer or a traditional tool.

Jules also leverages **natural language processing (NLP)** to interact with developers in a more intuitive way. When it analyzes a codebase, it's not just making technical decisions—it's also creating human-readable reports and pull requests. By understanding the structure of the code, Jules can generate explanations for why it's making certain changes, providing developers with clear and actionable feedback. This makes it easier for developers to trust and understand the AI's decisions, ensuring that they can remain in control of the process while benefiting from the automation Jules offers.

Once Jules identifies a problem, whether it's a bug or an optimization opportunity, it creates a **comprehensive plan** to fix the issue. Unlike basic tools that may only suggest a single line of code to change, Jules approaches the task from a holistic perspective. It considers how the fix will impact the rest of the codebase, ensuring that any changes it makes won't introduce new issues. This is where **Gemini 2.0's** advanced architecture plays a critical role, as it allows Jules to evaluate the overall structure of the code before making adjustments. It can even suggest refactoring strategies, ensuring that code is not only functional but also clean, maintainable, and optimized for performance.

When it comes to implementing fixes, Jules goes beyond merely suggesting changes. It autonomously prepares **pull requests**, making the necessary code modifications and offering them to the developer for review. This process, powered by its machine learning capabilities, allows Jules to implement fixes across **multiple files simultaneously**, ensuring that changes are made cohesively and efficiently. This multi-file approach is particularly useful in larger projects where bugs can be spread across different components of the codebase, and addressing them requires changes to more than one file or module.

By using machine learning and neural networks, Jules is able to solve complex problems, not just by understanding the code at a superficial level but by grasping the underlying logic and making intelligent decisions based on that understanding. It can also learn from feedback, improving its ability to fix bugs and optimize code with each iteration. This adaptive learning process ensures that Jules remains relevant and increasingly effective, making it a long-term asset for developers looking to streamline their workflows and enhance the quality of their software.

The power of **Gemini 2.0** and the sophisticated AI models behind **Jules** represent a leap forward in the world of coding assistants. Where traditional tools required manual input at every step, Jules can now take on the heavy lifting, allowing developers to focus on the bigger picture—innovation and creative problem solving—while leaving the repetitive tasks to the AI. By harnessing the power of machine learning, neural networks, and natural language processing, Jules is not just an assistant; it's a fully autonomous AI capable of transforming how software development is done.

Jules operates seamlessly within GitHub's ecosystem, a crucial platform used by developers worldwide to manage, track, and collaborate on their code. Its integration into GitHub is what truly sets it apart from traditional coding tools. Rather than requiring developers to leave their familiar workflow or jump between platforms, Jules embeds itself directly into GitHub, enhancing the way developers interact with their code. When a developer pushes new code or creates a pull request, Jules automatically takes action, analyzing the proposed changes and ensuring that no errors slip through the cracks. It functions not as a detached tool but as an active member of the developer's workflow, ready to assist at every stage without causing disruption.

As soon as the code is committed, Jules begins its analysis in real-time. It scans the repository, identifies potential issues like bugs, performance problems, or violations of coding best practices, and then offers detailed fixes. These fixes are not just limited to simple syntax corrections but can involve more sophisticated changes, such as refactoring code or optimizing performance. All of this happens without requiring any human input, allowing the developer to continue focusing on their higher-level tasks. Jules not only assists with bug detection, but it also proposes changes, creates pull requests, and prepares the code for review, essentially automating the maintenance side of development. The developer remains in control but can rely on Jules to handle the tedious tasks, streamlining the overall process.

This autonomy is what makes Jules so valuable. Unlike traditional tools that merely suggest fixes or highlight issues, Jules operates independently.

It doesn't wait for the developer to ask for help or issue commands—it proactively scans the codebase, identifies problems, and automatically implements fixes. This level of independence is made possible by the advanced machine learning algorithms and neural networks embedded in the Gemini 2.0 platform. These systems are designed to understand the structure and context of the code, so Jules can make informed decisions about what changes to apply. It learns from vast amounts of data, constantly improving its ability to solve problems quickly and efficiently. This means developers don't need to manually supervise or approve every small change. Instead, they can trust Jules to identify bugs, suggest fixes, and implement solutions autonomously.

This real-time problem-solving ability is one of the most significant advantages of Jules. In traditional software development workflows, identifying and addressing bugs can take considerable time. Developers need to write tests, run the code, debug it, and check for potential issues. This process can be slow, and even with the best intentions, bugs can sometimes go unnoticed, only to surface later in the development cycle. Jules changes all of that by instantly detecting problems as soon as they arise. Whether it's a syntax error, a performance issue, or even a security vulnerability, Jules identifies the problem and prepares a fix before the developer even notices it. This proactive approach helps eliminate the bottlenecks caused by debugging, reducing downtime and accelerating the entire development process.

Once Jules has detected an issue, it doesn't just flag it and leave it for the developer to deal with. Instead, it generates a detailed fix, one that is tailored to the specific context of the codebase. It considers the broader structure of the project, the dependencies between files, and any existing issues that might impact the solution. Once the fix is prepared, Jules creates a pull request, presenting the changes to the developer for review. This allows the developer to approve or modify the solution before it is merged into the codebase, ensuring that they maintain oversight without being bogged down by the repetitive tasks of debugging or testing.

Jules' real-time problem-solving is especially beneficial in collaborative environments. In team-based projects, multiple developers are often working on different parts of the same codebase at the same time. This can lead to conflicts when merging code, and bugs can spread unnoticed throughout the system. Jules acts as a safeguard against these issues, continuously monitoring the codebase for potential problems and fixing them as they occur. This proactive maintenance ensures that any changes made by one developer don't introduce unforeseen issues in other parts of the project. By detecting problems in real-time, Jules helps maintain the consistency of the code, reducing the likelihood of conflicts and improving the overall quality of the project.

In addition to solving problems as they arise, Jules' ability to work autonomously means that it can also improve efficiency by handling repetitive tasks that would otherwise take up a significant amount of a developer's time. From preparing pull requests to fixing simple bugs, Jules handles these tasks automatically, allowing developers to focus on more creative, high-level aspects of the project. By doing so, Jules helps optimize the workflow, ensuring that developers can deliver projects faster without sacrificing code quality.

Ultimately, Jules represents a significant leap forward in the way developers approach coding. Its deep integration with GitHub, its autonomy in managing bugs and code optimizations, and its ability to solve problems in real-time make it an invaluable tool for modern software development. With Jules working alongside them, developers can accelerate their development cycles, improve code quality, and focus on innovation—all while letting the AI handle the tedious, repetitive tasks. In this way, Jules doesn't just assist developers; it empowers them to work more effectively, ultimately transforming how software development is done.

Chapter 3: How Jules Works: Breaking Down Its Key Functions

Jules is designed to revolutionize how developers approach bug detection and fixing by automating the entire process. Traditionally, identifying bugs in software development is a time-consuming and often tedious task that requires developers to manually comb through the code, run tests, and debug issues. Jules, however, changes the game by performing this process autonomously and with remarkable speed.

When a developer pushes new code to the repository, Jules immediately gets to work. The first step in the bug detection process is **scanning the code**. Jules uses its machine learning algorithms to break down the code, identifying patterns and structures that may contain bugs or errors. It doesn't just look for syntax issues; it also considers the deeper logic of the code. This includes common bugs, such as null pointer exceptions, memory leaks, or logical flaws that might not be immediately obvious from a superficial review of the code.

Once Jules has completed its scan, it moves on to the next step: **evaluating the context** of the code. It's important to remember that code doesn't exist in isolation. There are interdependencies between files, functions, and modules. A bug in one area of the code could have ripple effects across the rest of the system, making it harder to pinpoint the source of the problem. Jules takes this into account by analyzing the **broader context** of the codebase. It examines not only the immediate file but also related files and modules, understanding how changes in one part of the code can impact others.

After identifying the issue and understanding its context, Jules moves on to **offering a fix**. Unlike traditional coding assistants that might only suggest changes, Jules autonomously **implements fixes across multiple files simultaneously**. This is especially useful in larger projects where a bug might span across different parts of the system. For example, a bug in a core module might affect the functionality of several other modules that rely on it. Jules doesn't just fix the bug in the initial file—it goes across the codebase to make sure the issue is resolved everywhere it has an impact.

Once the fixes are applied, Jules generates a **pull request** that includes all the changes. The developer can review the changes and approve them for integration into the main codebase. This process ensures that developers maintain control over their project while still benefiting from the automation that Jules provides.

Not only does Jules automatically fix bugs, but it also offers **optimizations**. As it analyzes the code, Jules looks for areas where the code could be more efficient. It checks for redundancies, performance bottlenecks, or areas where the code could be refactored to be cleaner and more maintainable. This is particularly useful when working on large, complex projects where technical debt can accumulate over time. Instead of relying on developers to catch these inefficiencies, Jules automatically identifies and offers improvements, ensuring that the codebase remains optimized and performant.

Jules doesn't just look for obvious errors—it also has the capability to **anticipate potential issues**. For example, if Jules detects that a function is underperforming or that a certain part of the code is likely to cause problems down the line, it will proactively suggest changes that prevent these problems from arising. This forward-thinking approach helps avoid future issues and keeps the project running smoothly.

The process of bug detection and fixing doesn't stop after one iteration. As more code is added or modified, Jules continues to monitor the repository for new bugs or performance issues. This means that the system is constantly improving and refining itself, learning from new data, and providing even more accurate and effective solutions over time.

Beyond bug detection, Jules is also designed to perform **comprehensive code analysis**. While bug fixing is an essential part of software development, the quality and efficiency of the code are just as important. This is where Jules really shines. Its ability to understand not just errors but also the **overall structure and health of the codebase** makes it an invaluable tool for developers seeking long-term improvements.

When Jules analyzes a codebase, it doesn't just scan for issues—it conducts a **holistic review** of the entire project. This includes looking at how different modules and functions interact with each other, how well the code adheres to best practices, and whether there are any performance inefficiencies. This is crucial because even if a project is free of bugs, there may still be underlying problems that can affect its scalability, maintainability, and performance.

Jules begins by **identifying redundancies**. Over time, software projects tend to accumulate lines of code that are no longer necessary, redundant functions, or overly complex logic that could be simplified. Jules can identify these redundancies and suggest more efficient ways of writing the code. For example, if a developer has written several similar functions that do almost the same thing, Jules might recommend consolidating them into a single, more efficient function. This reduces duplication, simplifies the code, and improves maintainability.

Next, Jules looks for **performance bottlenecks**. Performance is a critical aspect of any software project, and inefficient code can significantly slow down the development cycle or lead to slow applications. Jules uses its deep learning capabilities to identify areas where performance could be improved. Whether it's optimizing loops, removing unnecessary database queries, or restructuring logic to minimize resource consumption, Jules helps ensure that the code runs as efficiently as possible. This is particularly important for large-scale projects, where even small inefficiencies can have a significant impact.

Jules also checks for **adherence to best practices**. Writing clean, maintainable, and readable code is a key part of good software development. Jules analyzes the code to ensure that it follows industry standards and best practices. This includes things like proper variable naming, code formatting, and function modularization. By ensuring that the code adheres to best practices, Jules helps prevent technical debt and makes it easier for other developers to understand and work with the code in the future.

In addition to these checks, Jules also performs **security analysis**. Security vulnerabilities are a common issue in software development, and failing to address them can lead to severe consequences down the line. Jules scans the code for potential security flaws, such as SQL injection vulnerabilities, inadequate authentication, or improper data handling. By catching these issues early in the development process, Jules helps protect the project from future security risks.

Finally, Jules doesn't just identify problems—it also makes recommendations for improvements. These suggestions can range from small tweaks, such as reformatting code for readability, to more significant changes, such as redesigning portions of the code to improve efficiency or reduce complexity. By offering these recommendations, Jules helps developers continuously improve the quality of their codebase, ensuring that it remains scalable, maintainable, and high-performing as the project grows.

Jules' ability to analyze complex codebases and provide both bug fixes and optimization recommendations makes it an invaluable tool for developers at all levels. Whether they are working on a small project or a large, multi-faceted system, Jules ensures that the code is not only free of errors but also optimized for long-term success. Its comprehensive approach to code analysis goes far beyond just identifying bugs—it actively helps improve the quality of the entire codebase, making it easier to maintain, scale, and enhance in the future.

Jules takes the process of generating pull requests to the next level by automating and streamlining the entire workflow. In traditional software development, creating pull requests can often be a tedious and error-prone task. A developer typically needs to manually review the changes they've made, summarize the changes in a clear and understandable way, and then create a pull request that includes the fixes. With Jules, however, this process is automated in such a way that it removes much of the manual labor, ensuring that the pull request is both comprehensive and easy for the developer to review.

Once Jules has identified and fixed issues in the code, it doesn't simply apply the changes without explanation. It creates a **detailed, easy-to-understand pull request** that highlights all of the modifications made. These pull requests are designed to be clear, even for developers who might not be familiar with the specific issues that were fixed. Jules generates a full breakdown of the changes it has made, including descriptions of the bugs it found, how it solved them, and any improvements it applied to the codebase. This makes the pull request highly informative, reducing the time developers would typically spend reviewing the changes and allowing them to approve the fixes quickly.

Each pull request generated by Jules includes comments that explain the nature of the fixes and optimizations it has implemented. For example, if Jules fixed a performance bottleneck, it would provide an explanation of what caused the slowdown and how the changes improve the overall performance. If a bug was fixed, Jules would describe the issue in simple terms, outline how it was resolved, and offer any necessary context. This ensures that developers have a complete understanding of what has been changed and why, which is particularly helpful in team environments where multiple developers are working on different parts of the same project.

Moreover, Jules also tracks **dependencies between files**. If a bug is related to multiple files or requires changes in several areas of the project, Jules will take care of ensuring that all related files are updated accordingly. When generating the pull request, Jules automatically includes all the relevant files that were affected by the fix. This reduces the likelihood of errors or missed updates, ensuring that all necessary files are accounted for in one cohesive pull request. Developers no longer need to worry about whether they have missed updating an important file or whether a fix in one area could break functionality in another part of the project.

The pull requests Jules generates are structured in a way that fits naturally into the developer's workflow. Jules doesn't overwhelm the developer with unnecessary information or leave out crucial details—it provides exactly what is needed to ensure that the changes can be reviewed and approved efficiently. By creating clear, detailed, and well-organized pull requests, Jules reduces the friction that can often occur during the review process, allowing the team to move forward more quickly.

Another standout feature of Jules is its ability to work across **multiple files simultaneously**. In large-scale projects, bugs and issues rarely exist in isolation. A single bug can often affect multiple parts of the system, requiring changes across several files or modules. Jules is equipped to handle these complex scenarios by working across the entire codebase, identifying issues in multiple files at once, and fixing them without manual intervention.

When a developer pushes new code, Jules immediately begins its analysis. It doesn't limit itself to just one file or module; it looks at the **entire project** and identifies where bugs, errors, or inefficiencies might exist across different parts of the system. For example, if there is a bug in a core utility function, it may be used in multiple places throughout the project. Jules identifies these instances and makes sure that the fix is applied consistently across all files that reference or depend on that function. This is incredibly useful because it ensures that the code remains consistent and avoids the risk of introducing new bugs when fixing an issue in one file.

Jules can also handle situations where changes need to be made in several files that are interdependent. For example, if a change is required in a back-end module, that change might have a cascading effect on the front-end code or other connected services. Instead of requiring a developer to manually track all the affected areas, Jules automatically analyzes the relationships between the files and ensures that the necessary changes are made everywhere. Whether the issue is in one file or spread across dozens, Jules works across the project as a whole, making fixes in every relevant location and ensuring that the changes don't break other parts of the system.

This **multi-file fixing** capability is particularly important in larger projects with complex architectures. In such projects, manually identifying and fixing bugs across multiple files can be an incredibly time-consuming process. Jules simplifies this by automating it. By doing so, it not only reduces the time developers spend on bug fixing but also minimizes the risk of human error. When developers are required to fix issues in multiple places, there's always a chance that something will be overlooked or incorrectly implemented. With Jules, this risk is virtually eliminated, as the system takes care of updating every file that needs attention.

Once Jules has applied fixes across multiple files, it generates a comprehensive pull request that includes all the necessary changes. Each file that has been updated is included in the pull request, and the changes are all presented together, making it easy for developers to review. This ensures that nothing is left out, and the entire project is kept in sync. Developers can review the changes across the different files, approve them, and merge them into the main codebase with confidence.

By working on multiple files at once, Jules makes it easier for developers to handle complex projects with many interdependencies. It frees them from the task of manually tracking down issues in different parts of the code, ensuring that fixes are applied consistently and quickly. This automation allows developers to focus on more creative, high-level tasks while leaving the tedious work of bug fixing and code maintenance to Jules. The ability to manage multiple files at once also means that Jules can handle large projects efficiently, reducing the time spent on bug fixing and speeding up the overall development process.

In this way, Jules ensures that both individual bugs and broader code quality issues are resolved across the entire project, providing a seamless experience that enhances productivity and accelerates development timelines.

Chapter 4: The Integration of Jules with Developer Workflows

Jules fits seamlessly into a developer's daily routine, enhancing their workflow without causing any disruption to the tools and processes they are already accustomed to. One of the primary challenges for any new tool or technology is its integration into existing workflows, but Jules excels in this area by aligning perfectly with the tools developers use on a daily basis. Instead of requiring developers to switch between platforms or learn a new set of commands, Jules integrates directly into GitHub, the platform that most developers use to manage their code. This seamless integration ensures that developers don't have to interrupt their usual routine to benefit from the power of

Jules. Whether they are reviewing pull requests, pushing new commits, or debugging code, Jules is there, working quietly in the background, offering support without forcing developers to change their workflow or toolset.

When a developer pushes new code, Jules immediately kicks into action. It begins by scanning the code for potential issues, offering suggestions, and even implementing fixes autonomously. This happens automatically, without requiring the developer to initiate any specific commands or interact with an unfamiliar interface. Since it is embedded directly within the developer's familiar GitHub environment, it doesn't require the developer to switch tabs, open new applications, or manually trigger any processes. Jules stays integrated into the tools and systems the developer is used to, ensuring that the workflow remains uninterrupted.

Moreover, Jules works with existing processes and tools within the development environment. For instance, it respects the developer's preferred code standards, integrates with code linters, and works alongside version control systems like Git. Jules doesn't attempt to replace these tools; rather, it complements them by offering automated bug fixes, optimizations, and improvements, allowing the developer to stay in their familiar routine while benefitting from the enhanced capabilities that Jules provides. This makes it incredibly easy for developers to adopt Jules, as they don't need to abandon the tools they know and trust. Instead, Jules becomes an invisible, yet invaluable, assistant that operates behind the scenes, improving the development process without adding complexity.

Jules' integration also extends to collaborative environments, where multiple developers are working together on the same codebase. In such environments, consistency and synchronization are key. By working seamlessly within GitHub's workflow, Jules ensures that developers can continue to work on their individual tasks, while it takes care of identifying bugs, implementing fixes, and suggesting improvements across the entire codebase. The result is a smooth, efficient development process where developers don't need to constantly monitor every part of the project—Jules does that for them, handling the repetitive maintenance tasks while allowing the team to focus on the more creative and strategic aspects of development.

Jules also plays a critical role in **Continuous Integration (CI) and Continuous Deployment (CD)** pipelines, which have become essential for modern software development. CI/CD pipelines are designed to automate the process of integrating code changes and deploying them to production, ensuring that code is always tested, validated, and ready for release. However, maintaining a CI/CD pipeline that works efficiently requires a high level of coordination between different stages, tools, and processes. This is where Jules steps in, enhancing the CI/CD workflow by providing automated bug detection, code optimization, and fixes at every stage of the pipeline.

In a typical CI/CD pipeline, developers push their code changes to a shared repository, where automated tests are triggered to ensure that the code doesn't break anything. However, if bugs or errors are detected, developers often need to manually fix the issues before the code can move forward in the pipeline. With Jules, this process is automated. When code is pushed, Jules automatically scans it for issues, fixes any bugs, and generates pull requests for review. It then integrates seamlessly into the pipeline by pushing the fixes back into the repository, ensuring that the next stage of the pipeline—whether it's testing, staging, or deployment—can proceed without delay. This reduces the need for developers to manually intervene, speeding up the process and improving the overall efficiency of the pipeline.

Furthermore, Jules helps maintain the quality of code as it moves through the CI/CD pipeline. It doesn't just focus on bug detection but also looks for areas where the code can be optimized for performance, security, or scalability. As code passes through different stages of the pipeline, Jules continuously monitors it for any issues, offering fixes and improvements to ensure that only high-quality code moves forward. This proactive approach ensures that the final product is not only free of bugs but also optimized for production.

By automating the bug detection and fixing process in the CI/CD pipeline, Jules minimizes the risk of code issues slowing down development or delaying deployment. Developers no longer have to wait for manual reviews or spend time troubleshooting errors that could have been automatically addressed. Instead, Jules works in real-time to ensure that the code is ready for the next stage, keeping the pipeline running smoothly and efficiently.

In addition to improving the CI/CD pipeline itself, Jules also **supports collaboration** within teams by ensuring that the quality of code remains consistent. In a fast-paced development environment, where multiple developers may be working on different parts of the project, keeping track of code quality can be challenging. Jules ensures that code is continuously checked for issues, improvements, and optimizations, even as developers push new changes into the system. This helps maintain consistency across the project, ensuring that everyone on the team is working with clean, high-quality code that meets the same standards.

Jules also integrates seamlessly with automated testing tools commonly used in CI/CD workflows. As the code passes through different testing stages, Jules can automatically run tests, detect failures, and generate fixes. This further streamlines the process, reducing the manual work involved in testing and bug fixing. By automating these tasks, Jules ensures that the CI/CD pipeline remains efficient and that the team can focus on more valuable tasks, like feature development or enhancing the user experience.

The role of Jules in **CI/CD** extends to **continuous delivery**, where the aim is to make code changes available to users quickly and efficiently. Jules supports continuous delivery by ensuring that code is always in a deployable state. It fixes bugs, improves performance, and generates pull requests automatically, so the team can quickly move from development to testing, staging, and production without worrying about delays caused by manual interventions.

Jules also helps speed up the feedback loop in CI/CD. In a typical development process, developers often wait for the results of automated tests or manual code reviews before they can proceed with their next task. With Jules automating bug detection and fixes in real-time, the feedback loop becomes much faster. Developers can continue to focus on their next tasks while Jules handles the repetitive, time-consuming aspects of code maintenance. This means that code changes are reviewed, tested, and deployed faster, helping teams deliver features and updates to users more quickly.

By enhancing both the **CI** and **CD** stages, Jules accelerates development cycles, reduces the risk of human error, and ensures that code quality is maintained throughout the entire process. Its seamless integration into the developer's daily routine and the CI/CD pipeline makes it an indispensable tool for modern software development teams looking to streamline their workflow, improve collaboration, and deliver high-quality software faster.

Jules not only improves the technical aspects of software development but also enhances collaboration and communication within development teams. In a typical development environment, especially when multiple developers are involved, clear communication and coordination are crucial. One of the most challenging aspects of working in teams is ensuring that everyone is on the same page regarding code changes, bug fixes, and optimizations. Jules addresses this by making sure its actions and suggestions are communicated clearly and transparently to all team members, ensuring a smooth collaboration process.

In collaborative environments, **Jules acts as a mediator** between different developers, keeping track of changes, issues, and improvements across the project. When Jules detects bugs or makes improvements to the code, it provides a detailed, easily understandable summary of the actions it has taken. These summaries are automatically included in the pull requests it generates, making it simple for developers to see what has been changed and why. For example, if Jules fixes a bug, it provides a clear explanation of the problem, the steps it took to resolve it, and the impact of the fix on the codebase. This transparency ensures that all team members, regardless of their familiarity with the specific changes, understand what has been done.

Moreover, Jules doesn't just make changes silently—it actively communicates its reasoning. If Jules identifies a pattern in the code that can be optimized or a potential issue that could arise in the future, it suggests changes with full explanations. These suggestions aren't just technical jargon; they are designed to be **clear**

and understandable, even for developers who might not be intimately familiar with the codebase. By providing context for its actions, Jules helps the team understand why certain changes are necessary, fostering better collaboration and decision-making.

Jules also allows for **feedback loops** within teams. If a developer disagrees with a suggested fix or has additional insights, they can leave comments on the pull request, and Jules can adjust its actions accordingly. This creates an interactive, dynamic communication environment where developers can openly discuss and refine the changes being made. It also ensures that no important details or concerns are overlooked, as the pull request includes all relevant information about the changes and their rationale. As a result, the entire team can stay informed and engaged throughout the development process.

Another significant aspect of Jules' role in collaboration is its ability to **track dependencies across the codebase**. In larger projects, one developer might fix an issue in a particular module, which can have a ripple effect on other modules that rely on it. Jules automatically identifies these interdependencies and makes sure that the appropriate changes are communicated to all affected parties. For example, if Jules fixes a bug in the backend, it will notify the frontend developers if any adjustments are required on their end. This creates a coordinated, synchronized workflow where everyone is aware of how changes in one part of the system might impact other parts of the code.

Despite its autonomy, **Jules ensures that developers remain in full control** of the codebase. One of the key features of Jules is its emphasis on maintaining developer oversight, ensuring that human input is always valued and essential in the decision-making process. Although Jules can autonomously identify bugs, propose fixes, and even implement those fixes across multiple files, it doesn't take full control of the codebase without approval.

Before Jules merges any changes into the main branch of the project, it **requires explicit approval from the developer**. This ensures that the developer maintains control over what gets pushed to production. When Jules generates a pull request, it includes a detailed explanation of the changes made, any bugs fixed, and any optimizations applied. This information is easily accessible to the developer, who can review the proposed changes and ensure they align with the overall project goals.

The review process is designed to be **user-friendly**. Developers can quickly scan the changes made by Jules, read through the explanations, and approve or modify the pull request based on their preferences. This ensures that developers are never left in the dark about the changes happening in their project and that they can intervene if necessary. If a developer wants to fine-tune a fix or explore alternative solutions, they can do so without feeling pressured to accept the changes as they are. Jules' goal is not to override the developer's judgment but to enhance their workflow by providing detailed insights, suggestions, and fixes in a transparent and collaborative way.

Developers also have the ability to **reject or modify** the fixes suggested by Jules. If a developer notices something that doesn't align with the project's direction, or if they prefer a different approach, they can simply reject the pull request or suggest an alternative fix. Jules respects this feedback, learns from it, and adapts its suggestions accordingly. This ensures that while Jules works autonomously, it always remains aligned with the developer's goals and vision for the project.

This level of **control and flexibility** is crucial in maintaining a balance between automation and human oversight. Developers can rely on Jules to handle routine tasks like bug fixing and optimization, knowing that they still have the final say over what gets merged into the codebase. This not only boosts productivity but also provides peace of mind, knowing that they are never relinquishing control over their project.

In this way, Jules enhances collaboration by keeping everyone informed and involved in the process, while also providing developers with the control they need to ensure the project remains on track. By automating the tedious aspects of development—like bug fixing and code review—Jules frees developers to focus on higher-level tasks like feature development and system design, while still empowering them to make key decisions about the codebase. This collaborative environment, combined with user-friendly controls, makes Jules an indispensable tool in modern software development.

Chapter 5: Human Oversight: Ensuring Safety and Control

Despite its remarkable autonomy, Jules always ensures that **human developers maintain control** over every stage of the development process. One of the core principles of Jules is that, although it can autonomously detect bugs, analyze code, and suggest fixes, it never implements changes without the explicit approval of the developer. This guarantees that no modifications are made to the codebase unless the developer has reviewed and confirmed them.

When Jules identifies an issue, it works swiftly to craft a solution, but instead of immediately making those changes, it generates a **pull**

request. This pull request includes a detailed explanation of the bug, the fix applied, and any potential implications for the rest of the codebase. The developer then has the opportunity to review the changes, ensuring that everything aligns with the project's goals and coding standards. Only after the developer approves the pull request does Jules proceed to merge the changes into the main codebase. This built-in approval step ensures that **human oversight is always maintained**, providing an extra layer of confidence for the developer that the final code remains in their hands.

By requiring human approval, Jules establishes a **collaborative partnership** between the developer and the AI. While Jules handles the repetitive, time-consuming tasks of bug detection, code optimization, and basic fixes, the developer retains full authority over the final output. This autonomy for Jules allows for efficiency in the development process, but with the critical safeguard that human judgment is always a key part of the decision-making process. Developers can work more quickly, knowing that Jules will only make changes with their explicit consent.

To further protect the integrity of the codebase, Jules is equipped with a set of **safety protocols** designed to ensure that no unintended or harmful changes are made. These protocols are critical in maintaining the stability and security of the software project, particularly as Jules operates autonomously within the development environment. The goal is to make sure that while Jules can automatically detect issues and implement fixes, it does so in a way that avoids introducing new bugs, security vulnerabilities, or performance issues.

One key safety feature is Jules' ability to test any proposed changes before they are merged. When Jules identifies a fix, it doesn't just make changes to the code; it runs a series of **automated tests** to verify that the proposed changes will not break existing functionality or introduce new problems. This testing process ensures that any modifications made by Jules are thoroughly vetted and compatible with the rest of the project. Only after passing these safety tests will Jules present the changes to the developer for review.

Jules also has built-in safeguards that prevent it from making changes in certain critical sections of the codebase without additional validation. For example, if a modification could potentially affect core infrastructure or key functionality, Jules may require additional checks or review from other team members before proceeding.

This ensures that the system cannot inadvertently make a drastic change that could impact the overall stability of the software.

Moreover, Jules is designed to **track dependencies** between different parts of the codebase. If a proposed fix affects one module, Jules will check whether any other modules are dependent on it and ensure that those areas of the code are also updated accordingly. This prevents situations where a fix in one area could lead to breaking other parts of the system. Jules also notifies developers of any dependencies that could cause issues down the line, allowing them to make more informed decisions.

These **safety protocols** give developers peace of mind, knowing that even though Jules is working autonomously to optimize their code, there are multiple layers of protection to ensure that nothing unintended or harmful gets introduced into the system. The AI handles much of the work, but human developers are never left exposed to risk—they retain full control over whether or not changes are implemented and can intervene if something doesn't seem right.

The true power of Jules lies in its ability to foster **collaboration between humans and AI**, creating a perfect balance between efficiency and control. In the world of software development, AI has the potential to significantly speed up processes like debugging, code review, and optimization, but it is essential that developers remain in control, especially when it comes to complex decision-making and ensuring that the project's goals are met.

Jules helps developers work more efficiently by taking on tasks that would normally consume significant amounts of time, such as identifying bugs, fixing minor issues, and even proposing improvements to the code. By automating these routine tasks, Jules frees developers to focus on more **creative and high-level aspects of software development**, such as designing new features, solving complex problems, or enhancing the user experience. However, Jules never acts as a replacement for human input. Instead, it serves as a powerful **assistant**, making the development process more efficient while still allowing developers to make key decisions.

This dynamic between human and AI is a clear example of **AI-assisted collaboration**. Jules doesn't replace the developer but rather complements their skills, offering valuable support in areas where AI excels—handling repetitive tasks, quickly processing large amounts of data, and providing solutions based on patterns in the code. But, at the same time, the developer remains the primary decision-maker, ensuring that the project stays true to its vision and that code changes align with both functional and non-functional requirements.

Jules operates in a way that encourages **active collaboration** between developers and AI. Instead of pushing for complete automation, Jules facilitates an interaction where the developer can leverage the AI's capabilities while still having full oversight of the codebase. For example, when Jules identifies a bug, it presents the developer with a solution that can be reviewed and customized as needed. This allows the developer to learn from Jules' suggestions, refine them, and make adjustments to meet specific needs. Over time, this collaboration helps developers become more efficient in identifying potential issues, while still ensuring that the overall project vision remains intact.

Moreover, the **feedback loop** between human and AI is critical in maintaining the quality of the software. If a developer finds that a particular fix is not appropriate or that a suggestion doesn't align with the project's objectives, they can provide feedback, and Jules will adapt accordingly. This means that over time, the AI learns from these inputs, improving its suggestions and actions to better align with the developer's needs and preferences. It's not a one-way process where the AI dictates the changes; rather, it's a dynamic interaction where the developer and the AI work together to produce the best possible outcome.

Ultimately, **human-AI collaboration** creates a workflow that enhances productivity, reduces the likelihood of errors, and speeds up the development process. By automating repetitive tasks, Jules helps developers focus on higher-level thinking, while still ensuring that they retain complete control over the direction of the project. The result is a balanced, efficient, and collaborative development process that leverages the strengths of both human creativity and AI's processing power. With safety protocols in place and constant human oversight, Jules serves as an invaluable tool for modern software development teams, enabling them to deliver high-quality software more efficiently while maintaining control at every stage of the process.

Chapter 6: Real-World Applications: How Jules Is Impacting the Industry

In the world of large-scale software projects, bugs are inevitable. They can creep into codebases unexpectedly, often hiding in complex systems where multiple developers are working simultaneously. These bugs not only cause frustration but also slow down progress, introducing delays and additional costs. In one real-world example, a software development team at a tech company was working on an ambitious cloud-based platform. The platform was already live, serving thousands of users, but developers had been struggling with an ongoing issue—bugs in multiple sections of the code that were not only difficult to find but also complex to fix. The project had grown too large for the team to manually track every bug, and the sheer volume of issues made it feel like an insurmountable challenge.

That's when Jules stepped in. By integrating into their GitHub workflow, Jules automatically began scanning the codebase for potential bugs. It identified several issues that had gone unnoticed by the developers, ranging from minor syntax errors to more critical logic problems that could have caused system crashes. Jules didn't just stop at finding these bugs; it autonomously generated fixes for them, working across multiple files and modules. The developers were able to review the pull requests that Jules generated, where each bug fix came with a clear explanation and the necessary adjustments to ensure the code was working as intended. The fixes didn't just address the immediate issues but also optimized the system's performance in several places, which the developers had overlooked. What was once a daunting task, with bugs scattered across the project, was resolved in a fraction of the time, thanks to Jules' ability to work autonomously and simultaneously across multiple files. This saved the development team countless hours of work and allowed them to focus on new features and improvements instead of constantly battling bugs.

Another example of Jules' impact can be seen in the speed at which development cycles can be accelerated. In many software organizations, deadlines can be tight, and the pressure to deliver features quickly is constant. However, the need to fix bugs, optimize code, and ensure quality often causes delays, creating bottlenecks that slow down progress. In one case, a company that specialized in developing mobile applications for the retail sector had been facing significant delays in their development cycles. The team would spend weeks working on new features, only to be bogged down by recurring bugs and lengthy code review processes. The manual debugging process alone took up so much time that the developers found it difficult to keep up with the pace of feature requests.

With Jules integrated into their development workflow, the team saw an immediate improvement. Jules was able to automatically detect bugs as soon as new code was pushed to the repository, providing developers with suggested fixes in real-time. What used to take days of debugging now took just hours, and in some cases, Jules handled the entire process autonomously, requiring little to no human intervention. This not only sped up the development cycle but also improved overall team morale, as developers no longer felt the constant stress of dealing with recurring bugs. By automating these time-consuming tasks, Jules helped the team meet deadlines faster, push new features more frequently, and increase overall productivity. As a result, the organization was able to launch updates and new products at a much quicker pace, gaining a significant edge in a competitive market.

Improving code quality is another area where Jules has proven invaluable. In one case, a financial technology company was experiencing a recurring issue with the quality of their codebase. The team was growing, and with it, the complexity of the software. Over time, the codebase had become harder to maintain, with outdated practices and inconsistencies creeping in. Despite the team's best efforts, code quality had begun to deteriorate, leading to slowdowns in development and occasional bugs that affected users. This posed a real challenge for the company, as they were developing a platform that handled sensitive financial transactions, and every bug or inefficiency could lead to serious consequences.

Jules helped turn this situation around. The AI was able to analyze the entire codebase, not only identifying bugs but also pointing out areas where the code could be optimized for better performance and security. It suggested improvements in areas such as error handling, database queries, and security protocols, helping the developers modernize the codebase without having to manually go through each line of code. Moreover, Jules offered automated fixes for common issues like formatting inconsistencies and inefficient code patterns, which the developers could easily review and approve. Over time, as Jules continued to learn from the project and its context, the quality of the codebase steadily improved. What was once a slow, error-prone process was now faster and more reliable, with a significant reduction in bugs and performance issues. By improving code quality, Jules not only helped the developers build a more robust and secure platform but also ensured that future development could be done more efficiently.

Jules has made a profound impact on multiple industries, providing value to sectors ranging from **tech** to **healthcare** and **finance**, among others. In the **tech industry**, where software development is at the heart of almost every product, Jules is an invaluable tool for improving efficiency, reducing bugs, and speeding up development cycles. Tech companies—whether they focus on building cloud-based platforms, mobile apps, or enterprise software—can all benefit from Jules' ability to streamline bug detection and automate routine fixes, allowing their teams to focus on building new features and delivering value to users.

In **healthcare**, where software development is increasingly important for creating secure, reliable applications that handle patient data, Jules helps maintain high standards of code quality. Healthcare software must meet stringent regulatory requirements and security standards, and even small bugs or inefficiencies can have serious consequences. By automatically detecting issues and suggesting fixes, Jules ensures that healthcare applications remain secure, compliant, and functional. It can also improve the development cycle for healthcare companies by reducing the time spent debugging and optimizing code, making it easier to deliver innovative solutions to the healthcare sector more quickly.

The **finance** industry, with its highly regulated and data-sensitive nature, is another sector where Jules has a significant impact. Financial technology companies need to ensure that their software is secure, performs well under pressure, and complies with regulations. Jules helps these companies maintain code quality and security, particularly in critical areas like encryption, transaction processing, and financial reporting. By automating bug fixes and optimization processes, Jules reduces the risk of errors in financial applications, helping companies meet their strict deadlines and maintain the trust of their clients.

Jules is also a powerful tool for industries such as **e-commerce**, **automotive** (for vehicle software systems), **education**, and **telecommunications**, where software quality and efficiency are paramount. In these industries, the ability to quickly identify and fix issues in the code can make a significant difference in reducing downtime, improving user experience, and ultimately driving growth. As Jules continues to evolve, its applications across different industries are only expected to expand, creating a new standard in software development that emphasizes speed, collaboration, and quality.

In all these industries, the common thread is that Jules provides developers with a tool that enhances both the **efficiency** and **effectiveness** of their workflows. By reducing the time spent on repetitive tasks like bug fixing and code optimization, Jules enables organizations to focus on what really matters—delivering value to customers, enhancing user experience, and accelerating innovation. As industries increasingly rely on software to power their operations, Jules is poised to play a crucial role in shaping the future of development across the board.

Chapter 7: The Business Case for Jules

Automating repetitive tasks in software development, such as bug fixing and code optimization, brings about significant cost reductions for companies, especially those managing large-scale or long-term projects. These tasks, when performed manually, can be extremely time-consuming, requiring developers to invest countless hours tracking down bugs, resolving issues, and ensuring the system's stability. In many cases, these activities take away from time that could be better spent on building new features or enhancing the product. As a result, software projects can end up facing escalating costs, both in terms of time and resources.

Jules addresses this challenge by automating much of the bug-fixing and maintenance process. By scanning codebases for issues and implementing fixes across multiple files, Jules significantly reduces the amount of time developers need to spend on these repetitive tasks. Instead of manually identifying and correcting bugs, developers can rely on Jules to handle the bulk of this work autonomously. This frees up valuable time for developers to focus on more complex, creative tasks—like designing new features or addressing high-priority issues—without sacrificing the quality or stability of the software.

The time saved by automating bug fixes and code optimizations translates directly into cost savings. Projects that previously would have taken months or even years to complete can now be finished more quickly and at a lower cost. In addition to this, fewer bugs mean fewer support tickets, less post-launch debugging, and a faster release cycle, all of which contribute to a significant reduction in overall maintenance costs. By streamlining the development process, Jules not only improves efficiency but also allows businesses to achieve more with fewer resources.

Moreover, Jules has a direct impact on **IT project overruns**, a common issue that many organizations face when working on large-scale software initiatives. According to McKinsey's data, large IT projects typically run **45% over budget** and deliver **56% less value** than originally predicted. These overruns are often the result of unforeseen issues that arise during development, including delayed bug fixes, inefficient workflows, and the complexity of maintaining a large, evolving codebase. Projects that involve multiple developers or teams can quickly become bogged down by miscommunication, inconsistent coding practices, and delayed fixes, causing timelines to slip and budgets to balloon.

Jules directly addresses these problems by **optimizing the development process**. Through its ability to autonomously detect and fix issues, Jules reduces the risk of delays caused by bug fixing and code errors. By integrating seamlessly into the developer's workflow, it ensures that bugs are resolved promptly and without the need for excessive back-and-forth between team members. This speeds up the process of pushing updates, testing new features, and finalizing the project, ultimately leading to a reduction in development time and cost.

Furthermore, Jules' ability to analyze and optimize code quality from the outset prevents the accumulation of technical debt, a common contributor to project overruns. Developers are able to spot and fix issues early in the process, reducing the need for large-scale rewrites or troubleshooting at later stages of development. This proactive approach helps avoid the costly delays that often arise when issues go unnoticed until they become more complex and difficult to address.

In summary, by automating routine tasks like bug fixing and code optimization, Jules contributes to **substantial cost savings** across the software development lifecycle. The reduction in manual labor, faster bug resolution, and overall efficiency improvements lead to lower development costs and more predictable project timelines. When applied to large IT projects, Jules' automation capabilities address key challenges like **IT project overruns** by reducing delays, optimizing workflows, and ensuring that the development process stays on track. For organizations striving to stay within budget and meet deadlines, Jules offers a powerful tool that not only enhances productivity but also ensures that software projects are delivered on time and within budget.

As software development continues to evolve, the need for tools that streamline processes and enhance developer productivity becomes ever more crucial. In traditional development workflows, developers often find themselves caught in an endless cycle of debugging and maintenance, which, while necessary, can detract from the more innovative aspects of their roles. The ability to focus on high-level creative tasks—like designing new features, optimizing user experiences, and architecting systems—becomes harder to achieve when so much time is consumed by repetitive, routine debugging. This is where **Jules** steps in and revolutionizes the way developers work. By automating bug detection, fixes, and optimizations, Jules frees developers from the time-consuming task of manual debugging, allowing them to invest their time and energy into more valuable, impactful work.

The shift from reactive problem-solving to proactive development is one of the most significant advantages of using an AI like Jules. When bugs and issues are identified and resolved automatically, developers can spend their time writing innovative code, exploring new ideas, and enhancing the product. They are no longer bogged down by the task of chasing down every bug or trying to resolve performance bottlenecks in an inefficient way. By removing these roadblocks, Jules helps **boost productivity**, not only for individual developers but also for entire teams, as they can move faster, iterate more quickly, and push new features without worrying about the fundamental stability of their codebase.

This increased productivity translates directly into the return on investment (ROI) that companies experience when they adopt Jules. The traditional cost structure of software development often includes significant time spent on bug fixing and code reviews—activities that, while essential, don't always lead to visible progress. When a team is constantly bogged down by bugs, the overall timeline of the project expands, and resources are consumed in ways that don't directly contribute to the development of new features or innovations. By automating these tasks, Jules enables teams to reclaim lost time, which can then be reinvested into areas that drive **business growth** and **product evolution**.

To understand the ROI more concretely, consider the time savings Jules provides. Developers typically spend a substantial portion of their time troubleshooting and debugging. According to various industry reports, developers can spend anywhere from 20% to 40% of their time just managing bugs. In a large team of 10 developers, if each one is spending 30% of their time on bug fixes, that represents a significant drain on the team's collective productivity. With Jules handling a substantial portion of these tasks, that time is freed up for developers to focus on more complex, creative tasks, ultimately accelerating the development process.

Let's break this down in practical terms. Imagine a company with a development team working full-time on a software project. If the average developer's hourly wage is $50 and they're saving 30% of their time on bug fixes, this can lead to a **significant reduction in labor costs**. For example, if a developer saves 624 hours per year (as estimated earlier), and 30% of that time is spent on bug fixing, the company can save $156,000 annually just by automating that process. Over the course of a year, that's a **massive ROI** for the company, considering the minimal upfront cost of integrating Jules into their existing workflow.

But the impact of Jules on ROI doesn't stop with time savings. There's also the **cost of human error**, which is an inevitable part of manual debugging and code reviews. Developers, like anyone, are prone to mistakes, especially when tasked with repetitive, tedious tasks. These errors can result in bugs slipping through the cracks, issues going unresolved for longer periods, or even larger, more costly mistakes that require extensive rework. Jules eliminates this risk by consistently applying best practices, detecting bugs, and offering fixes based on its analysis, all without the errors that often accompany human involvement. This contributes directly to the overall **stability** and **reliability** of the software, reducing the likelihood of costly post-launch issues and support tickets that can drain resources.

The ability to mitigate human error not only helps with financial savings but also ensures that projects remain on track. In industries where deadlines and budgets are critical—such as in healthcare, finance, and technology—maintaining a stable, bug-free codebase can be a significant competitive advantage. By preventing errors from reaching production, Jules helps companies avoid costly delays, project overruns, and reputation damage that can result from bugs or poor performance. This, in turn, has a **long-term impact on the bottom line**, as companies that can release high-quality, stable software on time are more likely to attract and retain customers, avoid costly legal issues, and stay ahead of the competition.

Additionally, when a development team is relieved from the burden of manual debugging, they experience a **boost in morale and job satisfaction**. Developers are passionate about solving complex problems, building new features, and creating impactful software. But being bogged down by constant bug fixing can diminish their enthusiasm and creativity. By automating these processes, Jules empowers developers to focus on what they do best: building innovative products that push the boundaries of what's possible. This leads to **higher employee retention**, as developers are less likely to burn out or become frustrated with repetitive tasks. A more satisfied, motivated team is a productive one—and this contributes to a culture of success and long-term growth for the company.

For organizations seeking to **scale their development teams** without exponentially increasing costs, Jules is an ideal solution. Instead of hiring additional developers to handle the increasing complexity of a project, companies can rely on Jules to automate and streamline repetitive tasks. As the team grows, Jules ensures that the same level of efficiency and productivity is maintained without requiring a proportionate increase in human resources.

This allows companies to expand quickly, take on more projects, and deliver products faster, all while keeping costs manageable.

By automating time-consuming tasks and optimizing development workflows, Jules not only increases productivity but also ensures that organizations can scale their operations more efficiently. This creates an environment where companies can remain agile, adapt to changes quickly, and continuously innovate without getting bogged down in the mundane aspects of software maintenance. The ability to increase development capacity without the need for more human resources is a key differentiator for businesses looking to stay competitive in a rapidly evolving tech landscape.

In the end, the **ROI** for adopting Jules is clear: companies can save time, reduce costs, minimize errors, and ultimately deliver higher-quality products faster. By freeing up developers to focus on higher-level tasks, improving code quality, and reducing manual debugging efforts, Jules is transforming the way development teams work. In an industry where time is money, and quality is everything, Jules offers organizations a powerful way to maximize both.

Chapter 8: Ethical Considerations and Challenges in AI Development

As artificial intelligence begins to play a more integral role in software development, one of the key concerns that developers and companies must address is ensuring that **AI-driven fixes** are of the highest quality. While AI, including tools like **Jules**, can vastly accelerate the development process, the challenge remains of ensuring that these automated fixes do not introduce new bugs or degrade the overall quality of the software.

AI-driven tools like Jules can be incredibly efficient at identifying issues and implementing fixes across large codebases, but like any tool, they are only as good as the data and algorithms they rely on. Ensuring that AI-driven fixes meet the same quality standards as manual code interventions is crucial, particularly in complex or mission-critical systems where the consequences of even small bugs can be severe. AI systems learn from historical data and patterns, but they are not immune to errors, and in some cases, they may offer solutions that do not fully align with the developer's intent or the project's long-term goals. For example, a bug fix that works in one context might inadvertently break functionality in another part of the software, particularly when code dependencies are complex.

This is where **human oversight** becomes essential. While Jules can autonomously detect and fix issues, it still requires human validation before changes are merged into the main codebase. Developers must review the suggested fixes and ensure they align with the overall design and goals of the project. The role of the human developer, in this case, is not to manually fix the code but to **validate the AI's decisions** and ensure that they do not inadvertently introduce problems. By maintaining human oversight at every stage, companies can safeguard against potential issues and ensure that the fixes are not only effective but also maintain the integrity and quality of the software.

The concerns about trusting AI to manage software development processes are particularly pronounced in **high-stakes environments**, such as **medical software** or **financial systems**, where the consequences of failure can be catastrophic. In these industries, even small bugs or errors can have far-reaching impacts—ranging from financial loss to loss of life. When it comes to these critical applications, ensuring that AI systems like Jules can be trusted with code fixing and optimization becomes an important issue.

In the medical field, for instance, a bug in a healthcare management system could potentially lead to misdiagnosis, incorrect treatments, or the failure to deliver critical patient data on time. Similarly, in financial systems, a bug in a trading algorithm or transaction processing system could cause market disruptions or lead to significant financial losses. These sectors have stringent regulatory requirements, and software must meet high standards of accuracy and reliability.

While AI offers significant benefits in terms of speed and efficiency, organizations operating in these high-risk industries must take extra precautions to **validate AI-generated fixes** before implementing them. In many cases, this may involve using a combination of **automated testing**, **human review**, and **real-world simulations** to ensure that the AI's fixes don't introduce unexpected behavior or security vulnerabilities.

In addition, transparency in how AI tools like Jules work is critical in these environments. Developers and teams need to understand the reasoning behind AI-driven fixes and be able to explain them in plain language to stakeholders, auditors, or regulatory bodies. **Trusting AI** in such environments requires that companies take proactive steps to monitor the system's performance continuously, ensuring that any problems are detected early before they can cause harm.

One of the biggest misconceptions about AI tools like Jules is that they might eventually **replace developers** entirely. This, however, is far from the truth. Instead of replacing developers, Jules enhances and augments their capabilities. By automating routine tasks like bug fixing and code maintenance, Jules empowers developers to focus on more high-level tasks that require human creativity, judgment, and expertise.

In a typical software development cycle, developers often get bogged down by repetitive tasks that, while important, don't fully leverage their skills or expertise. By removing these time-consuming duties, Jules allows developers to spend more time designing new features, architecting systems, solving complex technical problems, and interacting with stakeholders. Essentially, Jules acts as a **force multiplier**, increasing the productivity and effectiveness of developers rather than replacing them.

Moreover, while Jules can handle repetitive tasks and make suggestions for fixes, it is still the responsibility of developers to make final decisions. **Human intuition and creativity** remain essential, particularly when it comes to understanding the broader business context, user needs, and long-term project goals. AI, no matter how advanced, still lacks the ability to make judgment calls that require understanding of **human nuance** and **strategic thinking**. Therefore, Jules enhances developers' abilities to deliver better software faster, without ever diminishing their role.

The rapid adoption of AI-driven development tools raises important **ethical considerations**, particularly in terms of **fairness** and

accountability. As AI systems like Jules increasingly make decisions in the development process, questions about transparency, bias, and responsibility become more pressing.

One key ethical concern is **bias in AI decision-making**. AI models, including those used in Jules, are trained on large datasets. If these datasets are not representative or are biased in some way, the AI might produce biased results. For instance, if an AI is trained on a dataset that doesn't adequately reflect a diverse range of coding practices, it might suggest fixes that work well for certain types of code but fail in other contexts. Similarly, if AI is used to automate code reviews or decisions about feature prioritization, there is a risk that these decisions could inadvertently favor certain perspectives or approaches over others.

To mitigate these risks, developers must ensure that AI systems are trained on **diverse, representative datasets** and continuously monitored for signs of bias. Regular audits of AI-generated code and suggestions should be performed to ensure that AI tools like Jules are producing **fair, unbiased outcomes** that align with the values of the organization and society at large.

Another ethical consideration is **accountability**. When AI tools are integrated into software development processes, it can become unclear who is ultimately responsible for the decisions made by the AI. If Jules autonomously fixes bugs or makes suggestions that lead to problems in production, who is held accountable? Is it the developer who approved the AI's suggestions? The organization that deployed the tool? Or the AI system itself?

To address this issue, clear **accountability structures** should be established. Developers and organizations must take responsibility for the outcomes of AI-driven decisions and ensure that there is **human oversight** at every stage of the process. This includes reviewing AI-generated fixes, testing them thoroughly, and ensuring that they align with the project's goals. Establishing a culture of **responsible AI use** ensures that developers can trust these tools without sacrificing their own sense of accountability and ethical responsibility.

In conclusion, while AI tools like Jules offer immense potential to revolutionize the software development process, it's crucial to approach their integration with a clear understanding of the challenges they present. From ensuring the quality of AI-driven fixes to addressing concerns around trust in critical systems and ethical decision-making, human oversight and accountability remain essential. AI does not replace developers, but rather augments their abilities, enabling them to focus on more valuable, creative work. By ensuring that AI systems are transparent, fair, and held accountable, we can harness the full potential of these tools while minimizing the risks and ethical concerns associated with their use.

Chapter 9: The Future of AI in Software Development: What Lies Ahead for Jules

As artificial intelligence continues to advance, so too will tools like **Jules**. The integration of AI into software development is still in its early stages, and as AI technology evolves, so will the capabilities of these coding assistants. One of the most exciting prospects for Jules is its ability to continuously improve and adapt alongside the needs and feedback of developers. Currently, Jules is already incredibly effective at automating bug fixes and improving code quality, but as AI becomes more sophisticated, it will only get better at understanding context, making nuanced decisions, and predicting issues before they arise. The idea that Jules could evolve to understand the broader goals of a project, adapt its suggestions to different coding styles, and even collaborate more seamlessly with developers is not too far from reality.

Evolving with Developers means that Jules will increasingly become more intuitive and attuned to the workflows and practices of individual developers and teams. Just as developers tailor their environments to fit their needs, Jules will learn to adjust its behavior based on the context of the project. For example, it could identify patterns in a development team's workflow and automatically suggest improvements or optimizations that fit the team's established practices. Additionally, Jules could use **feedback loops** to refine its capabilities, learning not only from successful fixes but also from mistakes or suggestions that developers reject. This continuous learning process would allow Jules to become more than just a tool—it could evolve into a valuable team member that grows alongside the developer's own skills.

Looking to the future, **predicting the next steps for Jules** is an exciting exercise. With advancements in machine learning and neural networks, the next generation of Jules could move beyond simply fixing bugs to also helping developers optimize the architecture of their code. Jules might begin analyzing the entire project's structure, suggesting ways to streamline it, refactor inefficient sections, or identify potential security vulnerabilities before they become problems. As the tool grows, Jules might also incorporate **user experience (UX) analysis** into its recommendations, advising developers on how to enhance the usability and accessibility of their software. In addition, Jules could learn to support a wider range of coding platforms and languages, making it a versatile tool that developers can use across multiple projects and technology stacks.

Another intriguing possibility is Jules' expansion into the realm of **collaborative development**. Currently, Jules operates as an autonomous agent within individual workflows, but as it evolves, it might have the capacity to assist teams in real-time collaboration, offering suggestions, coordinating fixes, and maintaining a smooth development process even when multiple developers are working on the same project. This could significantly improve coordination between teams, reduce conflicts between code changes, and help ensure that large-scale software projects stay on track.

The future of **AI in software development** is undeniably bright, and assistants like Jules will play a key role in this transformation. As AI continues to improve, we can expect it to become an increasingly integrated part of every development team. In the not-too-distant future, AI assistants will be ubiquitous across the industry, working alongside human developers in almost every coding environment. These assistants will not just help with bug fixing and code optimization—they will serve as co-developers, offering insights, managing code quality, and even anticipating potential problems before they occur. This shift towards AI-assisted development will likely lead to an industry-wide change in how software is built, with teams adopting AI tools as a standard part of their workflow, much like modern version control or integrated development environments (IDEs) are today.

As AI tools become more advanced, they will likely take on more responsibilities. Jules could evolve into a **full-stack assistant**, capable of helping developers with everything from backend code to frontend design and even deployment. It could integrate with tools like **CI/CD pipelines** and **cloud platforms**, automatically testing and deploying code as changes are made, all while maintaining the quality and integrity of the software. Moreover, AI assistants like Jules could help with more specialized tasks like **performance tuning**, **security auditing**, or even **compliance checks**, ensuring that code adheres to the latest industry standards and regulatory requirements.

In a **post-AI world**, where AI is fully integrated into software development, it's easy to envision a scenario where Jules and similar tools become **indispensable partners** to human developers. These AI tools will not only automate routine tasks but will actively assist in creative problem-solving, offering suggestions that a developer may not have considered, suggesting new approaches, and learning from the context of each project to enhance the final outcome. In this future, development teams might shift from simply coding to collaborating with intelligent systems that augment their expertise, transforming the process into a more dynamic and collaborative activity.

In such a world, software development would be significantly faster, more efficient, and higher quality, but there would still be an undeniable need for **human oversight and creativity**. Even in a fully AI-integrated environment, humans will remain essential for tasks that require intuition, empathy, and ethical considerations—such as designing user-centered features or solving complex problems that involve cross-disciplinary knowledge. Developers will continue to play the critical role of guiding the development process, making high-level decisions, and ensuring that the software being built aligns with the values and goals of the company, the users, and society at large.

In conclusion, as we look towards the future of AI in software development, it's clear that tools like Jules will continue to evolve, offering ever-more powerful features and increasing value for developers. AI-driven development assistants will help shape the future of software by increasing productivity, reducing errors, and accelerating innovation. However, while the technology will become more powerful and integrated into development workflows, the importance of **human judgment and creativity** will remain unchanged. Ultimately, AI tools like Jules will empower developers to do their best work, pushing the boundaries of what's possible while freeing them from the repetitive and time-consuming tasks that slow them down. As AI continues to shape the landscape of software development, it will be the **collaboration between humans and machines** that drives the industry forward into an exciting new era of innovation.

Conclusion

In conclusion, the advent of **Jules** marks a significant milestone in the evolution of AI-assisted software development. As an autonomous AI tool, Jules stands out for its ability to integrate seamlessly with existing developer workflows, offering real-time bug detection, automated fixes, and the generation of detailed pull requests. This deep integration within platforms like GitHub allows developers to stay focused on the creative and strategic aspects of development, while Jules handles the repetitive, time-consuming tasks of bug fixing and code maintenance. By learning from past interactions and continuously refining its performance, Jules is poised to become an indispensable tool in the hands of developers, helping them build software faster, with higher quality and fewer errors.

One of the key benefits of Jules is its ability to **autonomously identify and fix bugs** across multiple files simultaneously, all without requiring constant human input. This capability saves valuable time and reduces the risk of human error, allowing developers to focus on more complex, higher-level tasks. Jules' ability to analyze codebases, offer suggestions for improvements, and generate comprehensive, easy-to-understand pull requests is a game-changer for development teams of all sizes. Moreover, its built-in safety features and **human oversight protocols** ensure that developers retain control, making sure that AI-driven fixes are aligned with the project's goals and standards.

The integration of Jules into the software development process also brings about numerous **business benefits**. By automating routine tasks, Jules helps reduce development time and cost, leading to greater efficiency and faster time-to-market. With the ability to continuously improve and learn from its interactions, Jules is set to enhance productivity across various industries, from technology and healthcare to finance and beyond. The potential of this AI-driven tool is vast, and its future iterations could further expand its capabilities, making it an even more valuable asset to development teams around the world.

As we move forward in the rapidly evolving world of software development, it is essential for developers to embrace AI tools like Jules. The integration of AI into development workflows is no longer a futuristic concept—it is here, and it is transforming the way we write code. By adopting tools like Jules, developers can stay ahead of the curve, ensuring they remain competitive in an industry that is constantly pushing the boundaries of innovation. Embracing AI isn't just about automating tasks—it's about empowering developers to do more, work smarter, and create better software.

The future of software development is undeniably intertwined with the rise of artificial intelligence. As AI tools like Jules become more integrated into development workflows, they will not only help improve efficiency but will also pave the way for a new era of **error-free**, **innovative** software. Developers will no longer be bogged down by manual tasks like bug fixing and maintenance; instead, they will be able to focus on what they do best: creating, innovating, and pushing the boundaries of technology. The world of software development is about to become more efficient, more creative, and more impactful—and AI will be at the heart of this transformation.

Ultimately, the evolution of AI tools like Jules signals an exciting new chapter in the story of software development. With the right balance of **human creativity and AI-driven efficiency**, the future of development is bright, and the potential for innovation is limitless. It is up to developers, businesses, and tech leaders to embrace these changes, harness the power of AI, and shape the future of software development for the better. The journey is just beginning, and Jules is ready to lead the way.